# And Then There Were Five

Based on a true story

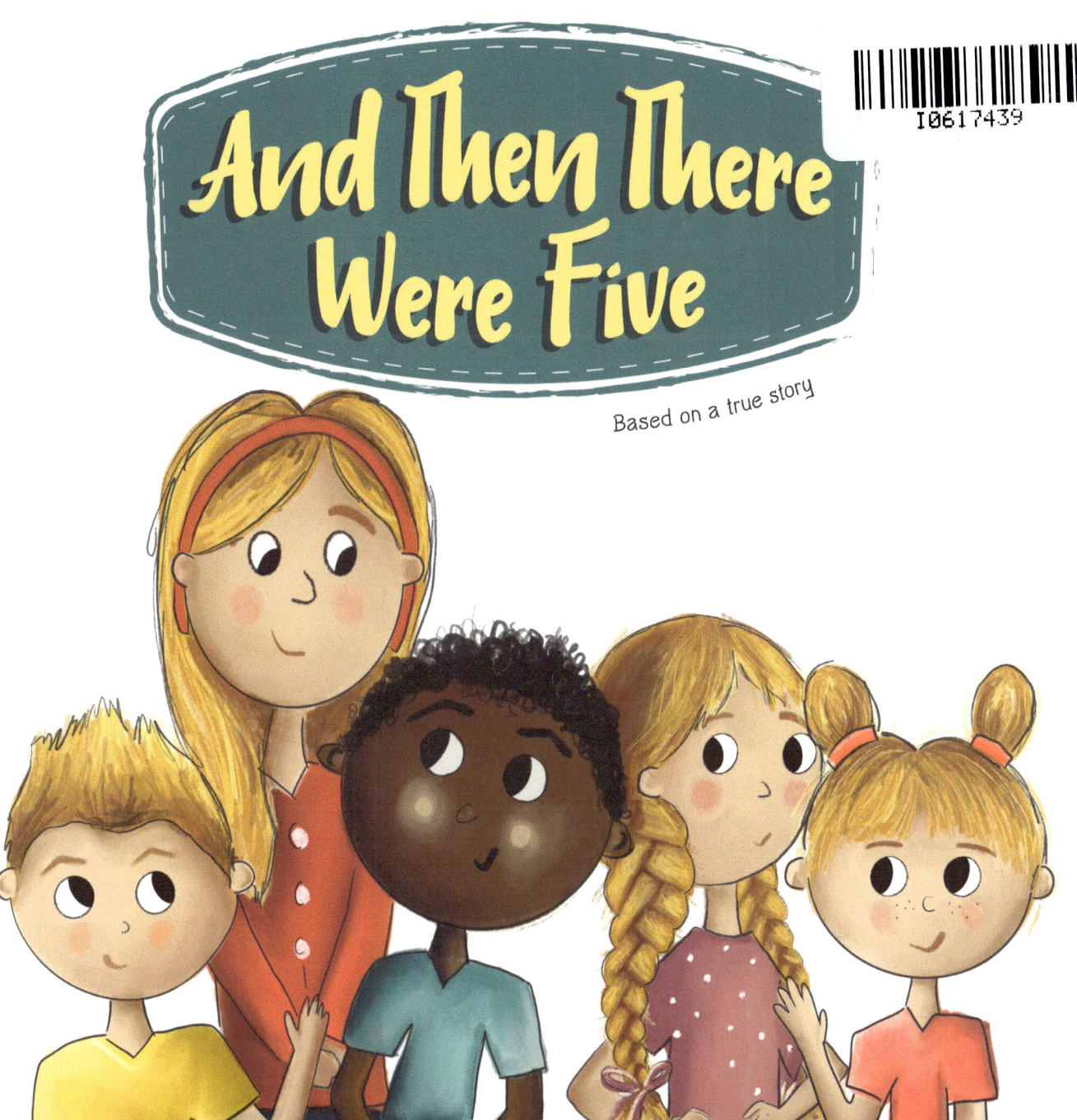

Crystal Anderson

Illustrated by Amy Fisher

I0617439

*And Then There Were Five* by Crystal Anderson.

All rights reserved © 2023. No portion of this book may be reproduced, stored in a retrieval system, or transmitted in any form or by any means, except for brief quotations in printed reviews, without prior permission from the author.

ISBN: 979-8-9894263-0-0 *(paperback)*
979-8-9894263-1-7 *(hardback)*

Editing, formatting, and cover design by ChristianEditingAndDesign.com.
Illustrations by Amy Fisher.

*Based on a True Story*

This book is dedicated to my family who loves me so well!

To my husband who challenges me to live beyond what I dare to dream
To my "4" who taught me that it is far greater to give than to receive,
and to my "1" who taught me that with God all things are possible.

And to my Lord and Savior, Jesus Christ, who doeth all things well.

"Maybe we should have more kids." Mom smiled at Dad. "The Anderson family only has four and has room for one more!"

Dad paused and thought for a moment. "Sure, let's adopt!"
"Adopt?" Mom gasped. "Now that I think about it, four is enough!"

But that night Mom thought about all the kids in the world who didn't have parents.
She prayed, "Dear God, do You want us to adopt?
Is there a child who needs a family just like ours?"

And in that sacred moment, Mom knew they were to adopt.
She could hardly wait to tell Dad and the kids.

Little did she know
In a faraway land
Was a sweet little boy
For whom God had a plan.

"Hey kids, come in here!" Dad motioned for them to sit on the couch. "Your mom and I have been thinking about something."

"This sounds serious," Nikki, the oldest sister, said to her siblings.

Dad continued, "How would you like to have a new brother or sister?"

Nikki rolled her eyes. "Mom! Are you having a baby?"

"Oh, heavens, no!" Mom replied. "We are going to adopt."

"Adopt?" Sam, the little brother, asked. "What's that?"

Dad placed his arm around his young son. "It means your new sibling is already born and needs a family."

"And we only have four and have room for one more!" Mom added.

The three sisters giggled at the thought of adoption. Ellie piped in, "I love babies and I'll help take care of her!"

"Oh yes!" Annie, the youngest sister, chimed in. "And I will help too!"

But they waited and waited and waited some more.
One year....Then two years....
Then three years went by,
and there were still only four and no more.

Until one day when everything changed.

Not just for Mom, Dad, and their precious four

But for the sweet little boy that would soon make one more.

"See that big plane, Rudy? We are going for a ride way up in the sky!"
Dr. Delaney pointed toward the clouds.

"To where?" Rudy nervously lifted his head to meet the doctor's kind eyes.

"We are going to fly on that big plane from Haiti to Georgia, where
doctors will help your heart get better!" Dr. Delaney touched the
young boy's shoulder. "Would you like that?"

HAITI

Rudy nodded. He was scared,
but God kept watch over him.

The Andersons were headed to Georgia too because Dad got a new job. It had all happened so fast, and moving day came quickly that cloudy May morning.

The three sisters agreed that the day seemed gloomy. They thought it might be because they said goodbye to their friends and their house for the very last time.

Mom counted the kids as they piled into the minivan.

One, two, three, four. There were still only four and no more.

Mom was so sad because she wished there were five.

But little did she know someone else was traveling too. On a big airplane way up in the sky was that sweet boy who none of them knew.

Rudy stared out the window as the plane landed. His mind raced with all kinds of thoughts: *I wonder what's going to happen to me. Will the doctors make my heart better? Who will take care of me?*

Rudy whispered a prayer. **"Dear God, give me a family that will love me just as I am."**

The Andersons arrived in Georgia too. When they pulled up in front of their new home on Mountain View Lane, the kids exclaimed, "Let's go find our new rooms!"

Nikki didn't have to share and had her very own room.
She peered out the big, beautiful window. "I like it!"

Ellie and Annie were very excited to share a large room
that had enough space for two beds and all their stuff.

Sam was last to find his room. He raced down the hallway
and hollered over his shoulder, "Where is it?" He stopped
when he saw it. "This is great! Look at my new room."

But something was missing. He thought to himself,
*If only I had a brother to share my space with.*

Summer went fast, and soon it was Fall.
But let me tell you the best part of all!

Another day came when something else changed. Dad called a family meeting and said to the kids, "We've met a ten-year-old boy from Haiti, and we want him to meet you."

"He's the same age as me?" Ellie looked around the room in disbelief.

"Yes!" Dad replied. "He moved to Georgia just like you did, so you know how he feels!"

The kids sat quietly, not sure what to think. Then Nikki's eyes filled with tears. "I bet he misses his friends like we do!"

The room got quiet again until Sam spoke up. "Let's do something fun when he comes over, like decorate cupcakes for Halloween!"

"Do they do that in Haiti?" Annie questioned as she looked for the globe to find where Haiti was.

Ellie looked over Annie's shoulder and shot back, "I don't know anything about Haiti and don't really care." She bolted out of the room, stomping her feet as loudly as she could.

The next day Rudy came over. He walked shyly into the house on Mountain View Lane.

"Hi!" Sam was happy to meet his new friend.

"Come on in!"

Rudy looked at Sam and instantly smiled.

Nikki whispered to Ellie, a little taken aback by this ten-year-old boy, "Does he know what we are saying?"

"This way, Rudy." Nikki waved her hand to show him instead of just telling.

He followed quietly, still surprised by all the kids he had just met and the new house he had never seen.

Rudy's eyes widened in surprise. His mouth fell open when he saw the long wooden table covered with so many yummy treats.

Candy and sprinkles
And orange frosting too.
Time to decorate cupcakes.
But would he know what to do?

Nikki picked up a plastic knife and scooped up a big glob of orange icing. "Look, Rudy!" She smiled and pointed to the cupcakes. "Get some icing to spread on your cupcake!" She showed him as she spoke so he would understand.

Ellie and Annie watched curiously. Annie whispered, "Do they eat cupcakes in Haiti?"

Rudy smiled sweetly at them and began spreading more icing on his yummy cupcake.

After all the cupcakes were decorated and eaten, the biggest sister showed Rudy to the living room. They all watched Lilo and Stitch, and then Rudy left.

But Rudy wasn't gone long. He came back the next day and the next day and the next day.

And Ellie girl had quite enough!

"When is he leaving?"
Ellie wanted to know.
"Oh, sweetheart," Mom said,
"He's not going to go!
We've decided to adopt him
And give him a home."

Ellie shook her head.
"How on earth can this be?
I wanted a sister,
And he is a 'he'!
And, Mom, don't forget,
He's the same age as me!"

No, no, she won't have it.
A new brother ... uh, no!
There's no way he could stay.
She wanted him to go!

But Rudy heard everything Ellie said. He stood there so sad and thought to himself, *I knew they wouldn't love me just as I am.*

He decided that it was time to go and wouldn't stay another minute where he wasn't welcomed. He looked around, quiet as a mouse, and slipped out the back door with no plans to return.

Dad looked around the kitchen. "Where is Rudy? Sam and I are going to throw the baseball in the backyard. We wanted him to join us."

"I don't know." Mom shrugged and called, "Rudy? Rudy?" Her heart pounded faster and faster as she wondered where on earth he could have gone.

Dad walked up the sidewalk in front of the house, but there was no sign of him.

Mom checked the house again and in a panic opened the back door to check the backyard.

She hurried up the hill to get a better view of everything around her. She reached the top and noticed a big hole that Annie and Sam had been digging. She gasped,
"Rudy! You scared me half to death! Come back inside!"

In his thick accent, he said,
"No, Ellie doesn't want me here."

He'd heard what Ellie had said.
  She didn't want him here.
She wanted him to go,
  And his eyes were filled with tears.

Mom wiped his tears and brought him back inside. She prayed that *Ellie girl* would accept her new brother.

Soon it was Thanksgiving, and Ellie spent more time with Rudy. She noticed how sad he was sometimes as he missed his own home in Haiti. She wondered how he felt about not being able to do all the things the other kids were doing at their age because of his heart condition.

"Rudy?" Ellie said one day.

Rudy looked up.

"I just want you to know I'm glad you're my twin brother." Ellie grinned. "We're the same age, and we can make new friends together at school and church!"

This time happy tears filled Rudy's eyes. "Thank you, Ellie," he said.

Christmas morning came. It was the most special Christmas ever!
Mom and Dad watched their five children tearing into their gifts
that had been neatly wrapped under the tree.

As they looked at each other with deep love in their eyes, they
didn't have to say a word. They just knew.... They knew that
although they were celebrating the birth of Jesus on this glorious
Christmas Day, they were also celebrating an answered prayer.

God's perfect plan
For their family
Was a fifth child
Named Rudy.

Crystal Anderson attended Liberty University and taught elementary and middle school. When she's not taking care of bookkeeping for Biblical Ministries Worldwide, she enjoys a ride to the mountains, reading, baking, and spending time with family. She blogs about faith, life, and cooking at That Mom blog. She and Scott, her husband of nearly four decades, have five children. Crystal's huge heart for adoption has proven that love is stronger than any differences. *And Then There Were Five*, which tells the story of how her family adopted their son, is her first children's book.

Amy Fisher lives in Lancaster, Pennsylvania, with her wonderful husband and their two precious young children. Originally from Pittsburgh, Amy grew up in a home that encouraged creativity in the arts. She has a Master's degree in Music Education and taught elementary music before staying home with her children. After this transition, Amy began pouring more into her art career and business as a freelance artist and illustrator. Her faith as well as her love for nature and color are evident in her art. She enjoys warm drinks, hammocks, bonfires, and traveling. Soli Deo Gloria.

To Mom and Dad—the sweetest and most constant cheerleaders. Thank you for always supporting, encouraging, and celebrating our dreams.

Pictured above:
Krysta, John Rudy, Joshua, Alyssa, Jessie

Portrait drawing by
Crystal's daughter-in-law, Caroline

www.ingramcontent.com/pod-product-compliance
Lightning Source LLC
Chambersburg PA
CBHW041606120626

46551CB00002B/324